NIGHT IN THE WADI

NIGHT

N THE WADI

BY DVORA BEN SHAUL

with photographs by Werner Braun
Layout and Design by Shirley Hirsch

 SABRA BOOKS · NEW YORK

SBN 87631-026-9
LIBRARY OF CONGRESS CATALOG CARD NUMBER 77-124121
PRINTED IN ISRAEL BY E. LEWIN-EPSTEIN LTD., BAT YAM
COPYRIGHT © 1970 AMERICAN-ISRAEL PUBLISHING CO., LTD.
ALL RIGHTS RESERVED

*This book is dedicated to
The Israel Border Police
who watched over me
while I watched the wadi.*

Preface

THIS BOOK is based on observations made in the Judean hills during a three year period. Our wadi, in fact, is not really one wadi at all but a composite combining the features of several wadis in the region, the most important of them being Wadi Fukine and Wadi Kabu, their springs and the lovely *cul de sac* into which the spring of Ras Abu Amar flows.

For twenty years these wadis were on the ceasefire line between Israel and Jordan and as such they were to all intents and purposes a "no man's land" where civilization made few inroads.

In the wake of the Six Day War in 1967, these wadis became a favorite spot for hikers and nature enthusiasts and are now a tourist attraction. Unfortunately, as a result of this invasion by man, great changes in the habits of the wild-life there have inevitably followed.

It is, perhaps, the very fact that they are doomed to disappear that make them a subject worthy of record.

Jerusalem, 1970

Night In The Wadi

THE WADI was old in the time sense of living things before the first animals came to live there. The wadi is older now, even in the time sense of places, and nothing much has happened to change it. True, the lion and the bear long ago disappeared from the area and the trees are the poorer for the lack of a chattering squirrel in their branches, yet the animals of Addulam live out their lives much as did their ancestors in long forgotten days.

People once lived in the wadi and for a time the animals retreated, coming only at night to forage in the fields and vineyards. The people are gone now and their village a ruin as once again the wild things have claimed the wadi for their own.

The Judean hills have since time immemorial been a refuge for the hunted, both man and animal, and in this sparsely populated region nature has applied severe tests in selecting those who will live there. Here are none of the more demanding species, for the animals of Addulam are a hardy lot, eking out an existence in a land of scarce foliage and scarcer water. Addulam is a land of rock and scrub, where life is a matter of wit or of strength and only the swift or the wary may escape sudden, merciless death.

But there is beauty here too, not the soft beauty of gentler climates, but the splendor of space, of sunlight and the silver shimmer of moonlight over the boulders.

The Sun slipped behind the hill and darkness had come, seeping up from the wadi floor and tinting the hills with an inky shadow. The noisy rock partridges had, for the most part, chortled their last calls and save for an occasional sleepy cluck from an over-anxious hen, the sun-loving animals had settled into their night quarters before Jackal woke up.

The den of the jackals, a low roomy cave overhanging the spring, was at the moment occupied by only one adult female. Last year it had been a crowded den, with her mate and three fat puppies vying for space under its crowded roof. But the pups had been weaned and were seeking their own future mates in the packs of the wadi. Her mate had died, bitten on the nose by a viper during a night's hunting.

This year she would take no mate. Perhaps next spring she would descend to the grassy wadi floor and there one would approach her with tentative paw-wavings and play. Then, if he was pleasing to her she would once again join in the stiff-legged mating dance, the frolicking and the mock chase before going off to start a new family with him.

But this year, driven by her instincts, she would remain alone, grieving the grief of the monogamous female for her lost mate in the only way she could, by denying herself mating and the bearing of pups for a season and giving the widow's haughty rebuff to any lone male approaching her, even in the mating season.

The spring moult had finished a few weeks before, and Jackal sat in the entrance to her den, grooming her silky new coat, running her tongue over flanks and shoulders and now and then using her sharp front teeth to nibble at a piece of briar or a bit of grass trapped in the densely packed hairs of her pelt. She was watching, too, looking out over the wadi in

wary preparation for the night's foray, now and again cocking an ear to catch a sound from down below.

Jackal heard the stirrings of the rodents among the fallen terraces. Some of them would serve as her supper tonight but as yet she was not anxious to eat. She heard the crashing in the underbrush as a hedgehog hurled his half kilogram body through a blackberry bush.

She had long ago ceased to tamper with hedgehogs or porcupines. As a pup she had tried, but a quill in the face is a painful thing and hardly worth the effort. Once, when very hungry, she had killed a hedgehog but the miniscule meal was small reward for the pain in her festered nose, pain from which she had suffered for more than two weeks.

From somewhere on the opposite slope

another jackal gave a tentative wail, and it was answered by others. The lone female joined in the rising crescendo and the wadi reverberated with the cries before they trailed off into a few staccato barks. Then there was silence again and from a terrace below she heard the thumping of an alarmed hare. This was a sound to conjure up the memory of many good meals, and Jackal stood up, taking a bearing on the sound and silently fading into the shadows as she went out to begin her night's hunt.

Hedgehog

Hedgehog also heard the thumping of the hare, but it didn't mean much to him. True, he had in the past succeeded in stealing a baby hare from the nest but this was a rare thing and could in most cases only happen by chance. Of greater interest was the scurrying of beetles and the squeak of baby mice under the terraces.

Crashing along in his armor of quills he blundered into the bole of a fallen olive tree and paused to see what obstacle blocked his path. Muttering the soft "chug-chug" which signifies hedgehog's annoyance, he set about with elephantine determination to try and shove it out of the way, and only after several minutes of vain struggle did he clamber awkwardly over the trunk, still muttering

and shaking his quills. Not once did he try to go around it, for such is not the way of the irascible hedgehog whose only route is as straight a line as he can follow.

Near the log a large scarab beetle was scuttling through the leafy mould, and Hedgehog, with a snap of his jaws, caught and ate him, scarcely pausing in the process as he meandered down the path to the spring. Near the spring would be more food; beetles and frogs and perhaps even a nest of baby mice, warm and pink without, as yet, the sleek mouse pelt of their parents.

On a high, flat rock just below the spring, Hedgehog caught the musky scent of a viper. Stopping dead still, he peered out beneath the crest of scowling quills on his brow and sought the source of the scent.

Seeing and hearing the viper slithering along the edge of the boulder, Hedgehog elevated all his quills, and at the sight of his traditional enemy made ready for battle.

Hedgehog lunged towards the viper. Feet, face and tender underbelly protected under his bramble coat, he charged head-on, giving the startled viper scarcely enough time to coil and strike. The slithering coils of a three-foot long viper pulled themselves into striking position and the hollow, needle-like teeth struck the hedgehog, embedding themselves harmlessly in the mat of quills as the deadly yellow venom spilled over the back of the aggressive assailant.

Again and again the viper struck, spurred on by the prickly assaults of the hedgehog, until after a dozen or more strikes, no venom was ejected and the viper was a harmless creeping thing seeking escape from certain death.

Only then did Hedgehog unfold his bowed body and with a swift, sure grip he caught the viper by the throat and with rapid sawing motions of his tiny, needlesharp teeth beheaded his adversary, a tiny David against a Goliath more than twice his weight.

Without further ado Hedgehog proceeded to make his meal from the still writhing body of the beheaded snake, sinking his teeth into the white flesh and making small smacking noises as he devoured his prey.

Hare, too, was enjoying her meal, not oblivious to her surroundings as was the hedgehog, sure of himself in his thorny mantle, but munching swiftly the fine green fern that grew in a clearing below the abandoned orchard. Once a dam had collected the water here in the days when man had been about, but now the dam was broken and the waters had abated.

The fragments of the old dam still held a small amount of moisture, making this spot flourish with fern and mushroom as well as succulent grass.

The Hare munched . . . and worried, nose a-twitch to catch even the faintest scent of a predator, long ears erect in perpetual alert. She had not lived almost three years and given life to more than a dozen bunnies by being a careless hare. Even now, heavy with a new litter, she was alert and agile, now pausing to listen, now to sniff the warm spring air. Once she crouched flat against a stone, aware of an owl flying high above the wadi. Her stomach almost full with fern and grass, she hopped aimlessly about looking for some last tidbit to finish her meal, when her keen restless nose caught the scent of Jackal coming from down wind and very close beside her.

She leapt. Pausing neither to look for her enemy nor to orientate herself, she ran, slipping automatically into the zigzag running pattern dictated, to the last detail, by inheritance. One jump right, two left, three right, one left and then repeat. The rhythm of the running pattern was in her very cells, and neither thought nor habit could change it.

Jackal, unable to turn as swiftly as Hare, was nevertheless at a distinct advantage as to length of stride. Down the slopes raced Hare with Jackal in hot pursuit. The clearing before them was growing less, and, from experience, Jackal knew that once among the blackberry bushes and boulders she would see no more of her quarry. In a desperate spurt of speed she gained the needed inches and her mouth grazed Hare's back at the exact second in which the hare froze. Motionless she stood as Jackal, carried by her own momentum and with far less "braking power" than the agile hare, raced on, tumbling onto the grass in an awkward sprawl as she tried to check her speed. The seconds gained while Jackal composed herself were all that were needed.

With a leap that cleared more than a yard, Hare was off again and into the protective shelter of a blackberry patch, where Jackal could never follow. Under the blackberry bush where the sweeping lower branches touched the ground, Hare sat, the fear of her recent encounter still upon her as she huddled motionless, ears flat against her body, heart pounding and muscles so recently stretched to the limit of endurance still twitching as they gradually returned to their accustomed relaxed readiness. At last she began to groom herself.

Her nose and nibbling lips passed over her

swollen flanks, heavy with pregnancy. In a few more days she would choose a protected spot amongst the boulders and there, in a shallow nest lined with grass and the hair pulled from her own chest and abdomen, she would give birth to her helpless litter, nourishing them with her rich milk and warming them during the cold nights with her body. Only a small percentage of her young would reach maturity, for the dangers facing the newborn hare were many. The snake that would swallow them whole while they were still helpless and blind, the cats, polecats, badgers, jackals, hyenas, owls and hawks that would comb the wadi by day and by night in search of food for their own hungry broods, all would take their toll. For the lucky survivors, each day would be filled with a dozen narrow escapes such as the mother's escape from Jackal this night. But survivors there would be, for such is the miracle of life, that a small brown hare, utterly without means of defense could live to the advanced age of three years in a world where there were no friends and only other hunted creatures were neutral.

Gazelles

On the upper terrace overlooking the eastern rim of the wadi the herd of gazelles was grazing. Here the grass was tender and plentiful, and among the stones at the edge of the terrace, grape vines, long grown wild, provided young shoots and leaves much loved by these small ruminants.

The spring night was warm and still, and only a small breeze stirred to carry scent or sound. The moon gave little light for it was waning now, a threadlike crescent of silver cupping the embryonic form of the new moon that would soon be.

Old "Crumple Horn", the oldest gazelle in the herd, stripped the luscious young leaves from the vine with practiced ease. She had fed in this place all her life. Ten springs had come and gone since the April day when she, newly-born and as yet unable to stand, had first opened her eyes in the abandoned vineyard just below. Now, in the spring of her eleventh year, she was the acknowledged leader of her herd and always the first to give the soft "snort" of alarm, a quick exhalation of breath through dilated nostrils that would immediately put the herd to flight.

Her place as leader of the herd was born of experience more than force. In her years she had survived drought and flood, fled from and outwitted hyenas, pariah dogs and men. Twice she had heard the crack of a poacher's rifle and seen another gazelle from her herd fall dying. She was wary, never resting from her endless guard. Her natural caution was reinforced by annual motherhood and she was suspicious of even common sounds. She was the mother of half the gazelles in the herd, including the male who was her mate. To most of last year's fawns she was grandmother.

A few hundred yards away in the middle of a shrubby grove, old "Crumple Horn's" three-day-old fawn was sleeping. The gazelle detached herself silently from the herd and picked her way to the almost unseen entrance between the bushes. She did not consciously hide her fawn from the other gazelles, but this was a precious secret, not to be shared. With a cautious glance over her back she disappeared into the shadows.

The new-born fawn lay curled up in the shadow of a boulder, almost invisible. "Crumple Horn" minced her way through the grass and nuzzled the sleeping fawn. The tiny gazelle jumped up on spindly legs and without a sound began nursing the rich warm milk, its black stump of a tail flicking from side to side as its mother bathed it with her moist tongue. In less than three minutes, having drunk its fill, the fawn was lulled by the mother's hypnotic stroking and, folding his legs, crumpled down in sleep, its stomach full.

The milk it had drunk, with twenty per cent butter-fat and virtually no sugar, would be digested slowly and the fawn would sleep until dawn when its mother would once again steal away to nurse it in secret.

Only after several days would the fawn be strong enough to forgo the passive form of defense in favor of swift flight. For now its sleepy invisibility was its only means of survival, together with the ever-present vigilance of its mother who would watch and guard and draw all enemies away from her fawn in swift pursuit, letting herself be nearly, but not quite, overtaken as she would lure them after her, eventually to lose them in the rocks and crags of the hillside.

Old "Crumple Horn" went silently back and rejoined the herd feeding on the terrace.

Stork

Stork was not born in the wadi. Three summers had come and gone since she had plummeted down from an autumn sky, her wounded wing hanging helpless as she fell. Now in the third migration season of her exile she was ready to return to her home in the northern part of Europe where she herself had been hatched, four years before. All week she had been restless with the urge to be off and away, and the coming of the great stork flight a few days ago had triggered a longing that could not be stilled.

The other storks, newly arrived from South Africa, were busy feeding on the grain, grubs and mice with which the fields above the wadi were filled. Their few days' rest were not enough to stoke the storage tissues of their slight bodies with energy for the thousands

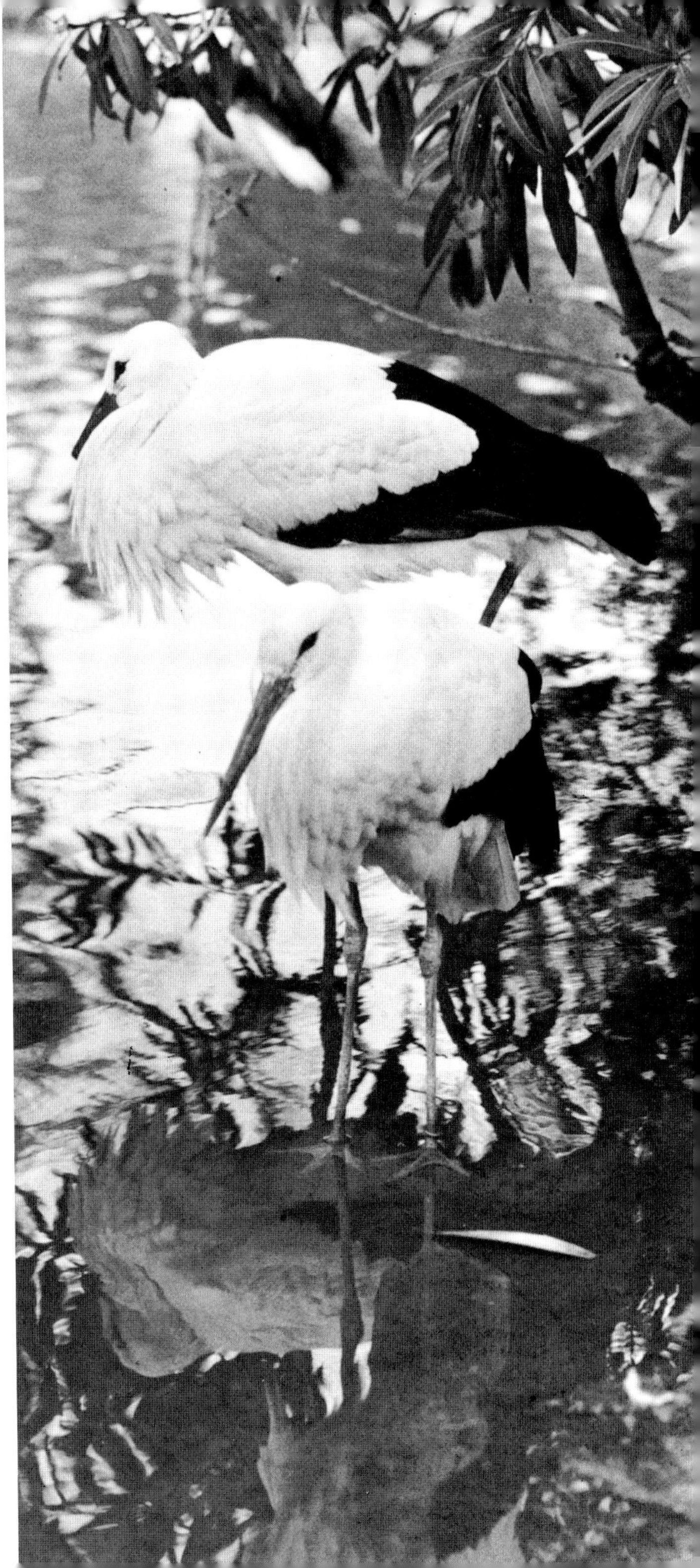

of miles that lay ahead. Resting and feeding, they were preparing for the next lap of their 8,000 mile migration, which they would repeat every year of their lives.

Stork was not depleted as were the migrators. For three years she had fed well and the wounded wing had grown strong again under the life-giving warmth of the Mediterranean sun. Each spring and fall she had been hostess to the flocks of her kindred and had stood with a lonely ache as they had soared away, her hunger for flight an hypnotic spell that fell over her when the season rolled round. But her helpless wing had allowed her only the small flight to a tree top to escape danger, and land-locked, she had stayed behind each time as the stork flight had winged its way high above.

In the early hours of dawn the storks, having rested and fed, begun to mill around in the field, orienting their awkward bodies towards the wind for the moment of flight.

Stork too was ready. Together with the others she flapped her wings and enjoyed once again the feeling of strength in their sinews. With a sudden heave, as if a signal had been given, the entire flight was off the ground and with a whirr of feathers in the wind was streaking upwards into the sky.

Now Stork was beautiful. Awkward and homely on the ground, in the sky she was splendid. Long neck stretched forward, lanky legs retracted, her strong wings stroked the spring air. The fields and villages streamed past below, tiny and insignificant from her haughty position. The wind played with her feathers and slipped unhindered across her streamlined shape. Stork was flying home.

Cat

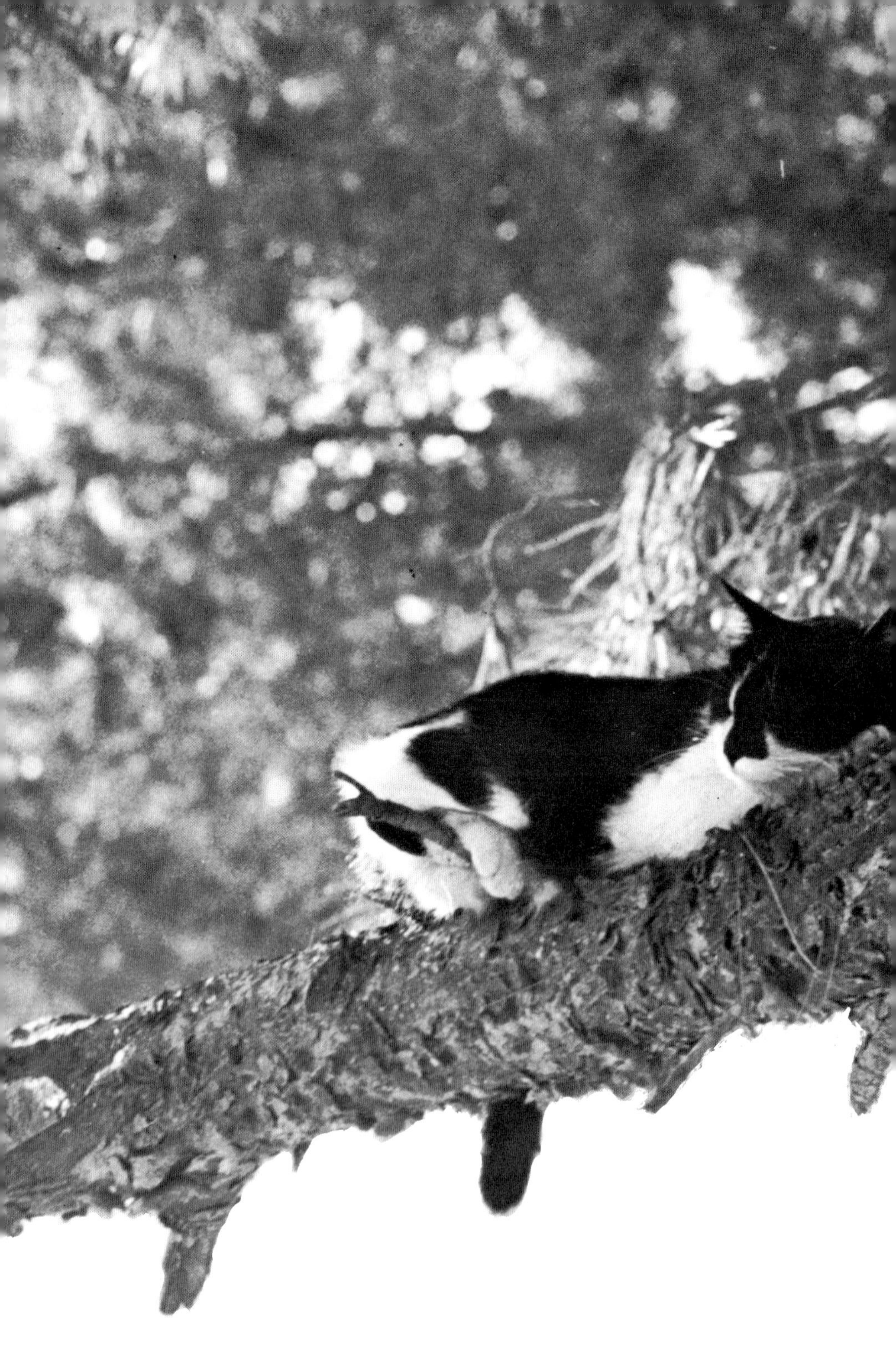

CAT WAS growing fat. Lean and hungry in the winter, driven by the urges of the mating season when he neither ate nor slept, when spring came he could relax. The sleek females were busy in their nests and dens giving birth to their kittens and Cat was alone. Mice were plentiful and the urgency of vanquishing his rivals no longer possessed him.

Slipping silently down the path from the spring, his stomach full, Cat caught the pungent odor of wild thyme. The essence stirred his senses and following the smell, Cat entered a clearing where thyme sprouted between the rocks. Sniffing the scented leaves, Cat rubbed his face against the plant. A feeling of intoxication came over him and he leapt into the air, a graceful arc of tawny fur in the moonlight.

Rolling and tumbling in the thyme, he crushed the leaves and the scent became even stronger. Cat was overcome by the heady perfume. He began to dance. Whirling and twisting in the moonlight he caught up a leaf and tossed it into the air, batting it with his paws and "killing" it in mock fury. Gliding through the bushes, as silent as his own shadow, Cat cavorted in the moonlight.

No house pet was this cat, nor was he a stray, feeding from trashbins, Cat was wild and his dance was the dance of the free cats that had always lived in the wadi and had played in the spicy thyme.

Cat began to purr, the sound of his contentment making a rumble audible from afar, but Cat feared no enemy in this wadi where he was king. Only Badger dared dispute passage with him on the game trails and these meetings Cat avoided if possible.

For almost an hour Cat capered in the clearing, then tired and drowsy he sat down beside the bush, washed himself from nose tip to the plume of his tail. Stretching his steel-spring muscles and yawning, he lay down, the scent of thyme in his nostrils. His tawny fur blended to perfection with the rocks among which he curled himself. Cat was still purring as he fell asleep.

Owl

OWL WAS TIRED. The night was yet young and already he had caught five mice and carried them to the nest in the cliff-face to feed the ravenous owlets. He was hungry, too, for not one morsel had he eaten for himself, and flying was hard work for a bird as big as Owl.

A week ago he had hovered nearby while his mate had ended her nesting weeks, and the four featherless owlets, born already hungry, had broken from their shells and demanded food. Together they had combed the wadi for enough to feed themselves and their hungry brood. The pickings had been poor in the wadi that week, for it was the time of the full moon when all hunted animals are especially wary. Driven on by the demanding cries of the hungry owlets they had flown far afield, even venturing into the planted fields nearby, where mice were plentiful. And plenty of mice were needed to supply the three pounds of food required to sustain themselves and their fast-growing family.

But in the planted fields of man where there were many mice, death was waiting too. Three days ago, his mate had eaten a poisoned mouse, and she was dead, together with one of the owlets with whom she had shared the food.

Left alone to feed and care for the three remaining nestlings, Owl was having a hard time. Last night he had been lucky and, sitting on a tree near the spring he had spied a plump young hare. Swooping down on soundless wings he had scooped it up before the hare had time to react. It had weighed more than a pound and afforded him a brief respite from his labors. But, tonight no hare was in sight and he must make do with mice, and mice meant forty trips or more across the wadi.

His great wings spread, Owl took advantage of the air currents and hoarded his energy

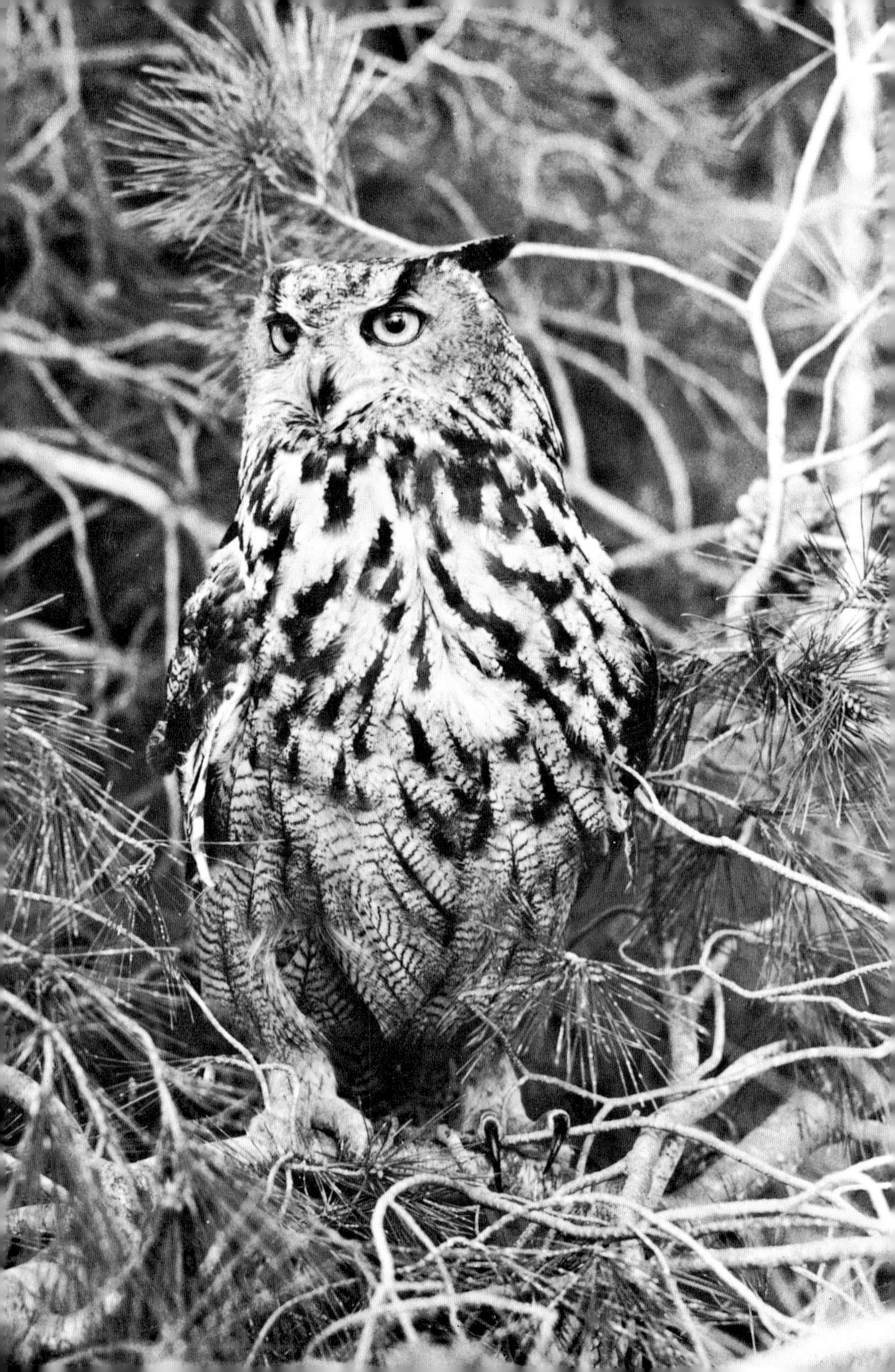

by gliding over the valley below, his big eyes seeking out the places where mice would be. Spying the bole of a fallen olive tree he descended and sat quietly waiting for a mouse to appear.

The mouse showed himself at the end of the log and Owl sat quietly. He didn't dare miss and therefore he was patient. When the mouse, lulled into security by the darkness and the silence, ventured out from the edge of the log, Owl caught him with his talons, killed him with a squeeze of his clawed foot, and hopped back onto the log. Overcome by his own hunger, he ate the mouse himself. Instinct told him that he must eat in order to feed the young, and already the three nights of deprivation had resulted in loss of weight and strength. Gulping the fresh warm flesh, Owl shook his feathers and once again was aloft, moving on to a new place. Luck was with Owl this night, and a meandering porcupine scared a brace of partridges from their place of sleep. One of them, a bit slower to dive for cover, was swept up by Owl and killed in his sharp claws. This was a real find, and although he was still hungry himself, Owl carried it at once to the nest on the rocky cliff.

At his approach, the owlets opened their beaks and screamed for food. Perched on the side of the nest, Owl tore the partridge into pieces which he stuffed into the gaping maws. Still unsatisfied, the owlets shrieked for more and Owl règurgitated the mouse he had eaten from his crop and fed them that as well. Now, hungrier and more tired than ever, Owl rested on the ledge, but the hungry cries of the nestlings spurred him on and once again he flew out over the wadi, his great wings beating slowly in the warm air as he sought more food to replenish his own strength and to silence his demanding youngsters.

In another night or so he would be driven by starvation to raid a farmyard for a plump chicken. Only desperation could overcome his fear and make him enter man's domain. If he was lucky, he would carry away a meal that would feed him and his brood for the whole night and then he would rest. If unlucky, he would be caught by man who would see in him only the chicken thief, little realizing that

Owl and his kind had long ago paid for the hen by their faithful service as rodent exterminators. Not yet desperate enough to steal chickens, Owl once more swung out over the wadi to hunt for mice.

Mouse

Mouse was small but she was brave. Twelve times already this night she had braced her trembling limbs and almost held her breath as she dashed out of her tunnel to gather a few more pieces of straw for her nest. With every trip her heart pounded against her heaving sides and her breath came in gasps as she braved the dangers of the trip. Now, with her thirteenth sortie before her, she paused at the mouth of her burrow, her long whiskers a-twitch as she peered out at the darkness.

A few yards away were some feathers left over from some long ago fox-feast and Mouse wanted them to line her nest. With her bright little eyes she looked out and her tiny cup-like ears were cocked to catch the smallest sound. Assured that all was still she bolted through the door, scuttling at once to the shelter of a bramble bush three feet away. There

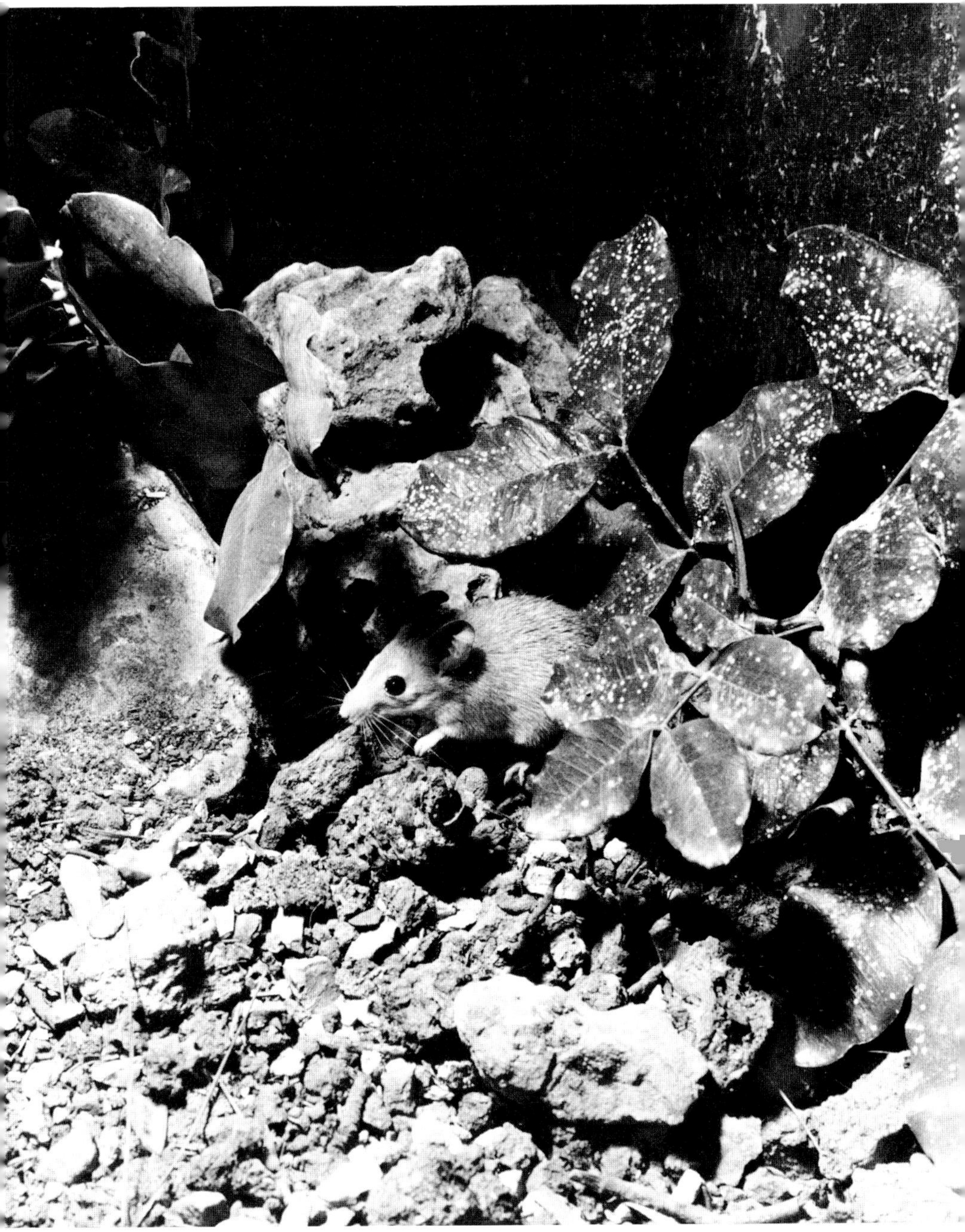

she examined once again the possiblity of danger outside and scurried to a large rock, pressing herself close within its shadow.

After four such leaps she reached the mound of feathers and began gathering them in her mouth, sometimes rejecting one for a better she had found. Her mouth filled with feathers jutting out at the sides, like a grotesque mustache, she ran. Not pausing for even an instant, she made a frantic dash to get back to the nest with her loot. A sound nearby made her drop her feathers and dash for cover under a stone. Quivering with excitement she peered out to see another mouse calmly gathering up her fallen plunder.

Mouse was furious. With a squeak of rage, she pounced out of her shelter and attacked the intruder, biting her severely and tumbling her about in the rustling leaves. Gone now was all fear. Only her precious feathers and her lost labors were important to her. The second mouse fought back but she was no match for the murderous attack and dropping her stolen goods she skittered away squeaking in terror. Mouse hurriedly gathered up the feathers and so intent was she, that she did not see the polecat until it pounced.

At the last second she sensed the danger and ran, the polecat almost upon her. Back safe under the bramble bush, she sat trembling, as the polecat, annoyed by its near-missed supper, sniffled around the edge of the bush.

Frightened, Mouse waited. After an interminable time, the polecat gave up and wandered off, looking for a more profitable place to hunt. When she was sure her enemy had gone, Mouse once again crept out of hiding, careful now with the memory of a near escape still freshly with her.

Gathering up the feathers for the third time, Mouse scampered off and dived into her tunnel with the materials still intact. In the den, she set about tearing them to bits with her sharp teeth and packing them in a fluffy layer in her nest. The plumes made a pile of soft material, but Mouse was not content. Somewhere in her mind was the memory of the mound of feathers she had left behind. Spurred on by the wish for more of this fine material Mouse, once again darted out of her tunnel.

Badger

BADGER WAS teaching her kittens the secrets of foraging for the first time, down by the spring where food was plentiful. The small black-and-white kits were three months old and Badger's milk had almost ceased to flow. The kits, unaccustomed to being out of the sett, were too full of wonder at the newly discovered world around them to learn much from their big mother this first lesson and were more absorbed in investigations of scents and sounds than in the more practical process of finding their suppers. Badger dug the rich soil away from a mass of tender roots and grunted a soft call to her playful offspring, showing them that these roots were indeed good to eat. The kits sniffed the roots and finding them a sorry substitute for the milk they had been allowed to enjoy until now, turned away from the repast with a snort that was only slightly short of disgust. Nonplussed, Badger waddled away in the direction of the spring. Keeping one eye open for any hint of danger to her kits she sat down to wait for a more tempting morsel with which to instruct her young.

Frogs were legion in the pools flanking the lip of the spring and soon after Badger sat down they were busy hopping about and making the night noisome with their raucous calls. Spying a large frog a few feet away, Badger tensed her strong body and with the speed of lightning bounded across the pool, catching the frog in mid-air as he leapt for safety a split-second too late. Carrying the limp frog in her mouth, Badger returned to the slope where her kits were still playing, their rough-housing and growls showing positive proof of their status in the wadi. Barring accident, the badgers were undisputed kings in their domain and had no fear of enemies.

Dropping the frog on the grassy slope, Badger once again called her kits and gaining their attention, tossed the frog to and fro, engaging the kits in play, that they might learn the movements of speed and stealth that would one day make them the most fearsome of all the foragers in the wadi.

Low-slung, overweight and pigeon-toed, the badger's stance belied the strength of their steel-spring muscles and the speed with which they could move. Confronted with a pack of dogs, the only foe capable of rousing fear in these staunch animals, a full-grown badger was capable of taking on six or more dogs and in the ensuing melee mutilating them all with his sharp teeth and iron claws.

The kits were more impressed with the frog than they had been with the roots and were easily persuaded to taste the meat as their mother rent the carcass and offered the morsels to the inquisitive youngsters. After the repast was finished Badger returned to the spring, this time trailed by her tumbling brood.

Badger hunted, the kits tagging along more interested in play than in their mother's activity. Now and again Badger called them to her, showing them the beetles, newts, mice, roots and berries that were good for food. At last, her hunger assuaged, she sat down to rest and the three kits crowded near, nuzzling her thick pelt in search of their preferred food. Nursing the cubs, the Badger sat a little longer to enjoy their presence before they would learn the lessons she had to teach and go off on their own to build their tunnels before the winter and the long rest began. In winter badgers, safe in their pelts and layered fat would sleep the long night away, rousing only once every few weeks to feed and then again to sleep.

Chameleon

CHAMELEON WAS already turning green. Curled under a bush, deep in his winter sleep, the small survivor of prehistoric times lay with his eyes open. Insensate and cold, only the photosensitive cells behind his retina recorded the changing scene and the pigments in his body responded, changing his color to maintain his camouflage even in the "little death" of hibernation.

No other creature so completely carries the song and the rhythm of the Judean hills in his very being as does this small reptile, for his kind are old, almost as old as the hills and wadis where he lives.

He was a contemporary of the great dinosaurs that once strode through this valley, and when the dinosaurs were gone and a newer, higher order had taken their place, the chameleon survived.

His requirements were modest, his camouflage superb, his life simple. A few insects for food, a handful of twigs for concealment and a bit of earth, moistened by the rain and heated by the sun to hatch the small white eggs that a new generation of chameleons might come into being. The seasons of the hills are the seasons of his life. The cold rain of winter brings rest, warm spring breezes wake him from his slumber, the hot summer sun invigorates him and the cooling days of autumn prepare him once more for the winter's cold.

He has survived millions of years of change. Neither climate nor predator has daunted him. A world has changed about him, yet he has lived on, as he has always lived, frugally, silently, harming no creature, save the insects on which he feeds.

Yet the days of the chameleon are numbered. The poisons absorbed in the insects he eats are already at work and each year fewer of the eggs are hatched. Rendered infertile by insecticidal sprays, the eggs remain in their burrow to rot away and no small, dragon-like chameleons scrabble their way through the hard-packed soil

Man is at last succeeding where fifty million years of natural disasters have failed.

Sleeping under his bush the chameleon is unaware of the handwriting on the wall.

Porcupine

Porcupine rattled his quills and sniffed the night breeze from the hills, lumbering along with a rolling gait. He had fed well this night for there were still tender twigs and mushrooms in the highlands and bulbs of spring flowers to be dug up in the wadi. Earlier he had gone up to the new-planted forests above the wadi and had feasted on the seedlings that man had planted there. Twenty or more of the tiny trees had made his meal and now, with stomach full, he ambled along, secure in his spiky armor.

The trap was placed across the game trail a few hundred meters from Porcupines' burrow. It was baited and fresh cabbage sent its scent into the air. Porcupine wrinkled his nose with pleasure at the sight of this delicacy. Porcupine knew about traps. He was seven years old and had been the enemy of man, the tree-planter, all his life. Nothing man could devise was new to him any more. He was cautious but stubborn like all of his kind.

Walking around the trap, he eyed the contraption from all sides and then sniffed at the door but made no move to enter. At last he approached the trap from the side and with great patience began to burrow under the trap. Using his strong forelegs with their sharp claws, Porcupine dug at the stony soil. Kicking the loosened earth behind he deepened his burrow under the trap until he could insert his head under its side. With a heave he gave a push upwards and turned the trap which was more than twice his weight onto its side.

The bottom of the trap was made of wire mesh as were its sides, but the bait lay on the floor tied to the spring that would release the door. Porcupine began pulling the cabbage leaves from between the metal wires. It was a slow way to eat but Porcupine never hurried. Leaf by leaf he pulled the bait from the trap and savored its moist freshness. At last, the cabbage consumed, he shook his quills and ambled off.

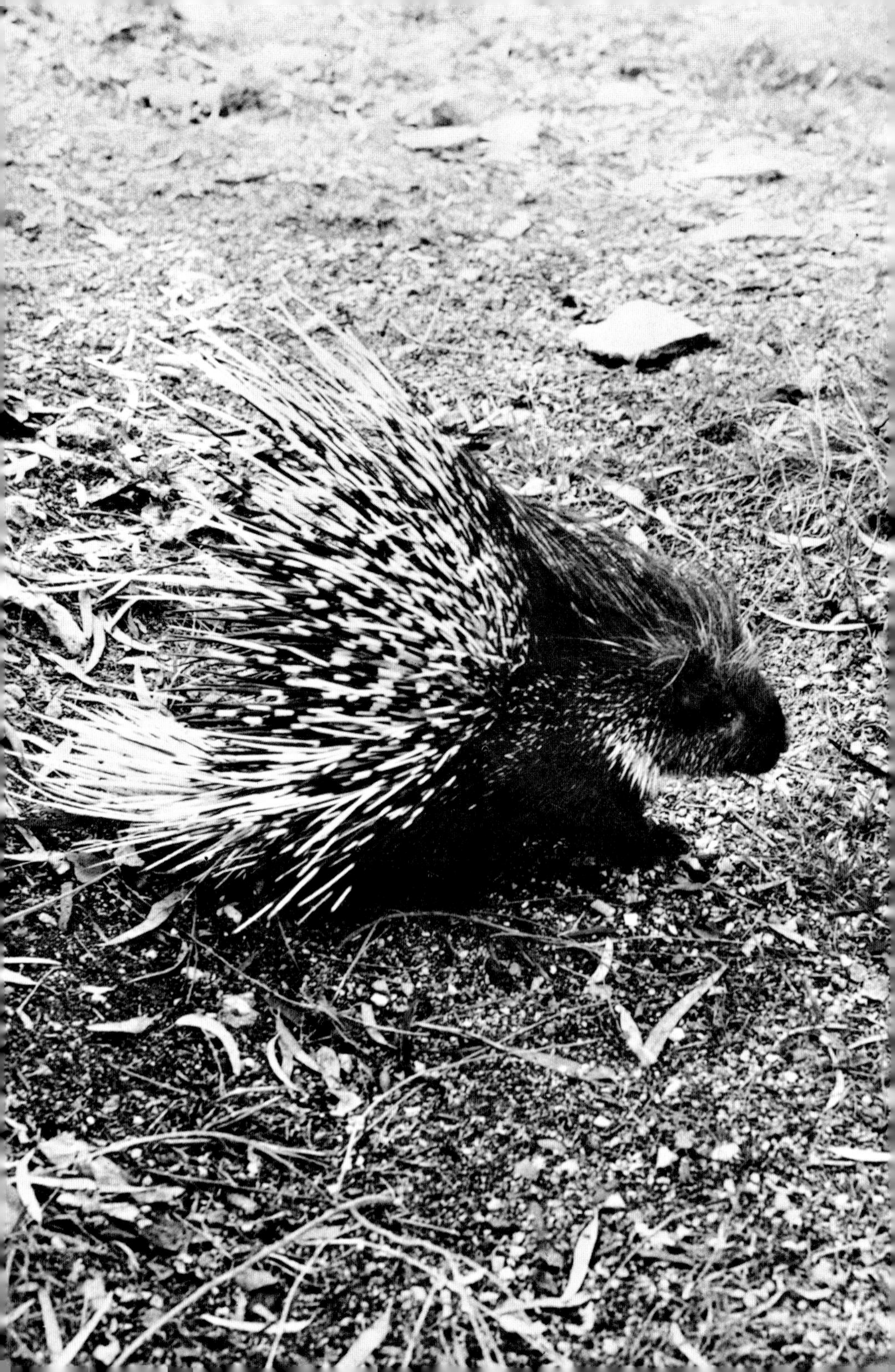

Several times more, he stopped to eat a twig or to investigate a new scent before he reached his burrow. The first rays of sunlight were already streaking the skies when Porcupine finally crawled head-first into his narrow tunnel and prepared himself for the day's sleep from which he would awaken the next night to go out and seek more trees, more mushrooms and perhaps even another cabbage, provided by the forestry service.

Eagle

SERPENT Eagle sat on a rock, his huge talons gripping the still lively snake he had just caught. With his sharp beak he beheaded the serpent and began stripping the succulent flesh from its body. He was not hungry, for this was the third coin snake he had caught today. He took his time, pulling delicately at the firm white threads of muscle and pausing now and again to clean his beak on the rocky outcropping of the boulder. Finishing his meal he flapped his great wings and was off in the direction of the nest in the crown of a half dead pine tree where his mate sat on their smooth, warm egg. It was time now for him to relieve her so that she too could hunt.

Approaching the nest from the direction of the wadi, his legs pumping in rhythm to the

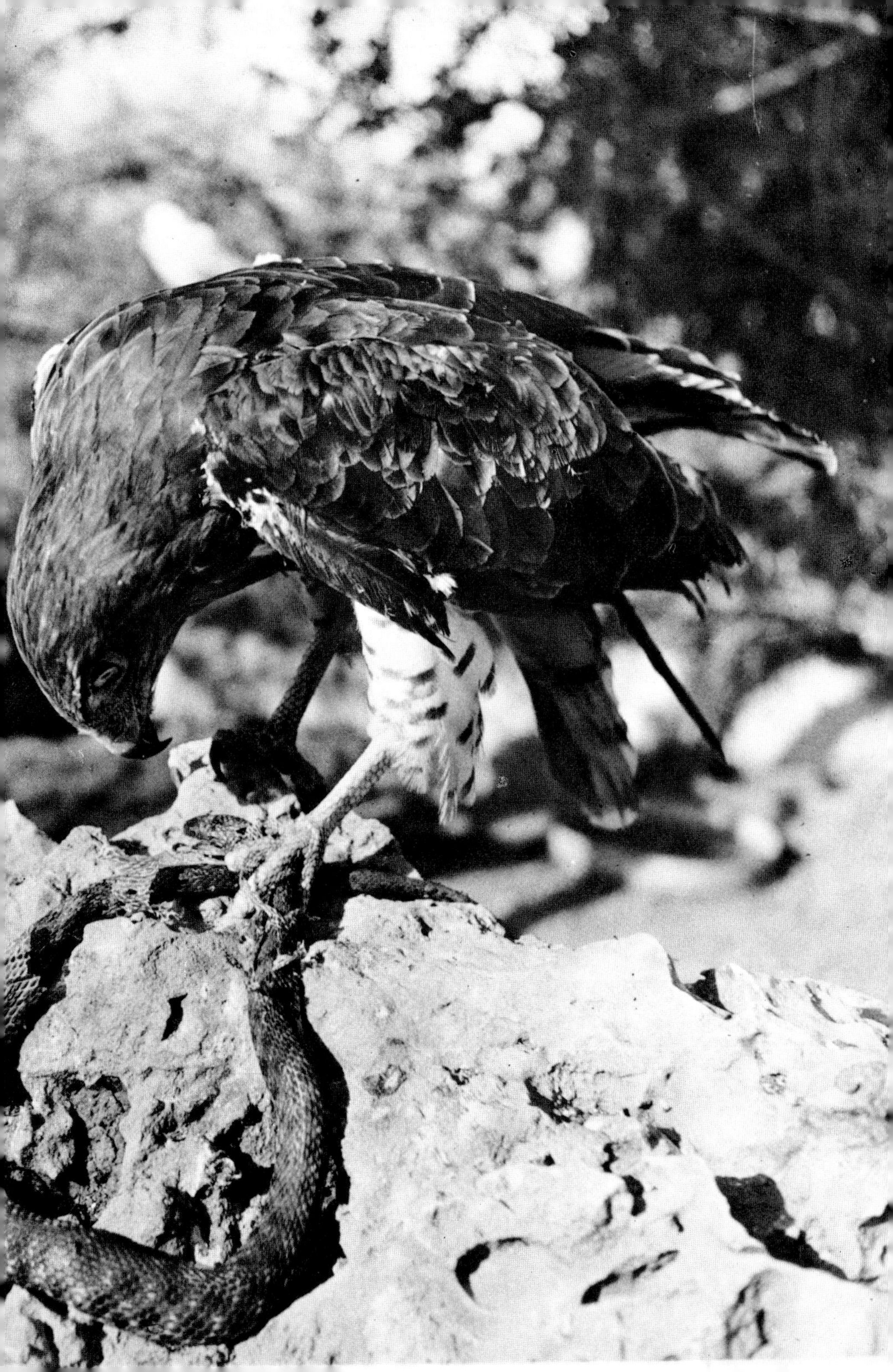

strokes of his wings in the distinctive flight pattern of his species, he uttered a fine-drawn, piercing cry to his mate. The female rose up from the nest at once and made way for him, greeting him with a swift peck of welcome as he took over the nest with its precious burden.

Settling into the large circle of piled twigs, Serpent Eagle rearranged a small branch and then, with talons so strong they could rend a hare in two swift strokes, he picked up the paper-shelled egg and turned it over, yet made not even a mark on its delicate surface. Eagle settled down in the nest, the warm sun and the nesting impulse that was sent out by his glands made him drowsy and he sat nodding in the spring morning. The feel of the egg nestled under his body gave him pleasure.

For yet another week the eagles would devote all their time to the important business of incubating their egg, for this was the vital period in the cycle of their year. In former years they had nested here and each spring had reared a hungry eaglet; feeding it with the food they hunted in the wadi and warming its fat, downy body at night with their own feathers.

This year there would be no nestling. Eagle did not, indeed could not know that for more than a year the snakes on which he and his mate had subsisted had been feeding on mice poisoned by man in the course of agricultural development. These poisons, not strong enough to harm Eagle or his mate were enough to pass over into the egg and the evil burden was already at work on the embryo.

For a time, after the appointed days had passed, the eagles would continue to nest until the urge was altogether gone and they would abandon their fruitless task to roam the wadi in search of food. They would be more energetic than usual in their hunting, for their instincts would drive them on to catch the prey that would feed their non-existent offspring.

Not knowing that he sat in vain, Serpent Eagle drowsed in the sunlight; even as the eaglet, poisoned before it was even conceived, died in its shell.

Fox

THE FOX-KITS, all three of them, were asleep. All night they had whimpered plaintively as they tugged at their mothers teats, where little milk was to be had. Accustomed to the unfailing supply of nourishment, the kits could little understand what was happening. They only knew that they were hungry and that there was no food.

Vixen slowly disentangled herself from the sleeping kits. Each movement was an agony and had been so since she had come home three nights ago, bleeding and in pain. She had gone out as usual to hunt for food that would nourish her own thin frame and provide milk for her three fat, hungry kits. Hunting had been poor in the wadi and at last she had climbed the hill to the planted fields where mice were plentiful and the furrowed earth gave good concealment for a huntress in the night. She had fed well and was just skirting the edge of the settlement when a farmyard dog sensed her presence and gave tongue.

Blinded by fear, Vixen had fled, racing across the field she had not even seen the coiled barrier of barbed wire until she felt the bite of its prongs in her flesh. The dog still barked and Vixen had no way of knowing that he was chained. Terrified, she struggled to free herself from the cruel barbs, ripping great gashes in her shoulders and flanks with every lunge. Free at last she had staggered back to her earth, weak with terror and with pain. Since then she had lain, exhausted and feverish, as her wounds festered and the hungry kits drained the last of her milk.

Now she must have water. All this night she had suffered the torment of thirst and her sure instincts told her that without food and water she and her kits would surely die. A dozen times she had tried to leave her den but her young were awake and fretful. They were too small to accompany her to the spring

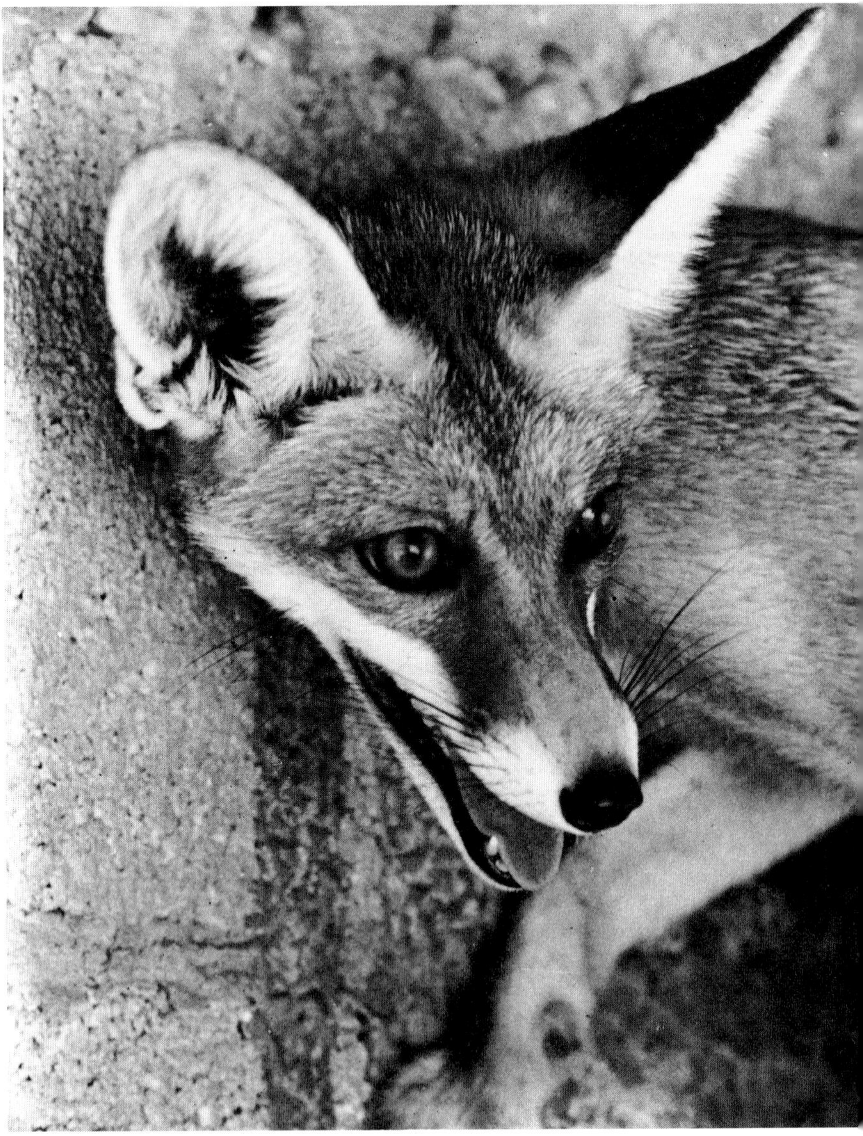

and she feared to leave them awake lest they try to follow and be lost on the way.

At last, exhausted in their struggle to get milk where none was to be had, the kits had fallen asleep and Vixen could leave her earth. It was half a mile to the spring and her right foreleg was useless but she must have water now.

Limping along on three legs, each step sent a shock of pain through her whole body. Three times she lay down along the way, too exhausted to go further but the will to live, and the thought of the spring ahead drove her on.

When Vixen reached the spring she was at the limit of her endurance. Falling down beside the waters edge she let the cool liquid flow passively over her sharp muzzle and into her parched mouth before she even began to lap from the pool. When her thirst was slaked she slid over the embankment and immersed her aching body in the flowing stream, wincing as the icy water laved her fevered wounds. Pulling herself from the pool she rested quietly for awhile and then got up, stretching her aching muscles by walking slowly about on the sun-drenched hillside. She was hungry but so foreign to her was the idea of hunting by day that she almost failed to see the partridge in front of her.

The Partridge was drowsy with nesting. The brooding urge had narrowed her world, telescoping it in on her eggs and nest and her self-containment blotted out the world around her. She neither saw nor sensed the prowling vixen until her life was snuffed out by a snap of quick jaws.

Vixen ate the partridge at once and then proceeded to the nest, breaking open the eggs and lapping up their contents. She finished them all and could have eaten more but her hunger was somewhat sated and a great drowsiness came over her. Pulling herself into the tall grass Vixen curled her tawny body into a ball, her bushy plume hiding her face, and went to sleep.

She slept all day. Her damp pelt dried slowly and the evaporation cooled her skin, drawing the fever from her wounds. Three days and nights of deprivation had taken their toll but she was strong and even as she slept her milk began to flow again.

It was the pressure of the milk in her dugs that woke her and though still hopping on three feet, Vixen wanted to get back to her earth and her young. Pausing only for one more drink from the spring she hurried home where the hungry kits were waiting.

Tortoise

Tortoise had not slept well this night for the stones around him had held the heat and the night air was warm, preventing the stupor that came to his cold-blooded body when temperatures were low. By the time the morning sun was high in the sky Tortoise was already half way to where he was going.

He was the oldest living inhabitant of the wadi and only he could have remembered, had his brain been indeed capable of such a mnemonic feat, the days when there had been a village with people in this now forsaken place. Because he was a reptile and his brain had developed in the oxygen-poor environment of a sun-incubated egg he lacked the ability to remember a great deal. Only a few things had he learned in his more than ninety years and one of them was how to get to the spot where he was now headed, a place where wild sweet-peas always blossomed in the spring.

Down the slope lumbered Tortoise, his short, scaly legs scrabbling along the stony path as he dragged his bony carapace over the uneven terrain. It was a long journey but at last he reached the spot where the wild legumes grew in abundance. Tentatively he clipped the blossoms with his horny, beak-like mouth. His thick, short tongue pressed the petals against his palate and he savored their juicy sweetness. Together with wild melons and a few berries these blossoms would form the staple of his summer diet.

Finding no more blossoms within easy reach, Tortoise began looking above his head, tempted by the lush clusters of flowers that waved in the breeze just out of his reach. One clump, close to a boulder, caught his fancy and bracing his back legs firmly, he scrabbled up the side of the boulder, his long neck outstretched as he reached for the coveted cluster. Losing his balance he fell from his ungainly perch and rolled over and over down the slope, coming to rest upside down on the curvature of his carapace, his stumpy legs flailing in the air.

When he was younger, Tortoise had been terrified when he landed like this and it had taken him hours or even days to get himself upright again. Years of experience had taken the terror from the situation and he was long an expert at turning himself over again. Twisting his flexible neck about he looked around until he saw a rock that promised a likely place to turn over and still on his back he began to rock himself from side to side like a capsized boat, his sharp claws coming briefly in contact with the earth on each sideways roll. Using his claw tipped feet like oars, he slowly inched his way to the stone. In half an hour he had covered the foot and a half that separated him from his salvation and reaching up with his right forefoot he gained a purchase on the stone, then mustering all his strength, he flipped himself over with one gigantic heave. Once more on his feet, he retraced his way to the spot from where he had fallen and once again climbed up to reach for the tantalizing treat. This time he did not fall and the prize was his.

Not two yards away, deep in a mound of earth and leaves that lay piled under a carob tree, a clutch of leathery tortoise eggs were slowly being incubated in the sunshine. These were his children but Tortoise was unaware of this; nor was the female with whom he had mated, and who had laid the clutch, any longer concerned with their existence. Once she had dug the hole, laid the eggs and covered them carefully she had gone her way and for her they were no longer a responsibility. The warm sun and the heat given off by the decaying vegetable matter would finish the job and the tiny tortoises, exact replicas of their parents would emerge, already able to fend for themselves. This in itself was one of the wonders of their kind, for even now, inside their leather walled prison, the tiny turtles were recapitulating stages of evolution that had taken place when the world was young.

At first a fish-like creature with a straight spine and customary ribs, the embryos under the direction of their inheritance would begin to grow their armor plates; the forming of the carapace would bring about structural changes, drastic in their design. Legs would splay outwards, spine would fuse to the carapace and the ribs would flatten like pickets in a fence, making necessary a way of breathing unlike any other animal. At last, misshapen and awkward, the tiny tortoises would emerge,

clad in an armor that, barring accidents, would serve them well for more than a hundred years. Thus had every tortoise developed throughout the millions of years.

Tortoise, unaware of his role in this evolutionary spectacle, and oblivious to the drama being enacted under the carob tree, waddled off in search of a new cluster of blossoms.

Jay

JAY HAD never been so angry in all her life. Only yesterday she had finished building her nice new nest. Tirelessly she had woven into the twigs the bright bits of string and the fleece stolen from a sheep in the meadow above the wadi rim. In irritation, she had scolded her mate as he tried to help and brought all sorts of unsuitable materials to the nesting site. Finally she had finished and the construction was well secured and hidden in the topmost branches of a giant pine. Only this morning she had laid her first egg in the fleecy bowl.

Leaving the nest, she had gone to eat for she would not begin to sit on the eggs until the last of her clutch was laid a few days from now. She had fed on grubs and berries down on the wadi floor and now, returning happily to her tree she saw the Spotted Cuckoo sitting on the nice new nest with a complacent air as if she and not the jay had built it there.

Cuckoo was not only sitting on the nest. She was laying an egg in it. The product of some evolutionary idiosyncracy, Cuckoo, like all of her kind, had no instinctive knowledge of nest-building, brooding or the rearing of the young. Yet nature had decreed that her kind should survive and so she used the nests of other birds, laying her eggs there and abandoning them that another species might hatch and rear the young cuckoo. Even should she remain within a few dozen yards of the parasitized nest, never would she attempt to feed her infant, nor would she acknowledge it in any way.

Shrieking with fury, the blue-gray jay dove at the cuckoo, striking with her sharp beak and flailing with her wings. At the edge of the nest she caught a limb of the tree with her feet and beat wildly at the usurper. Her screams rent the morning air and the tree-top trembled with her onslaught.

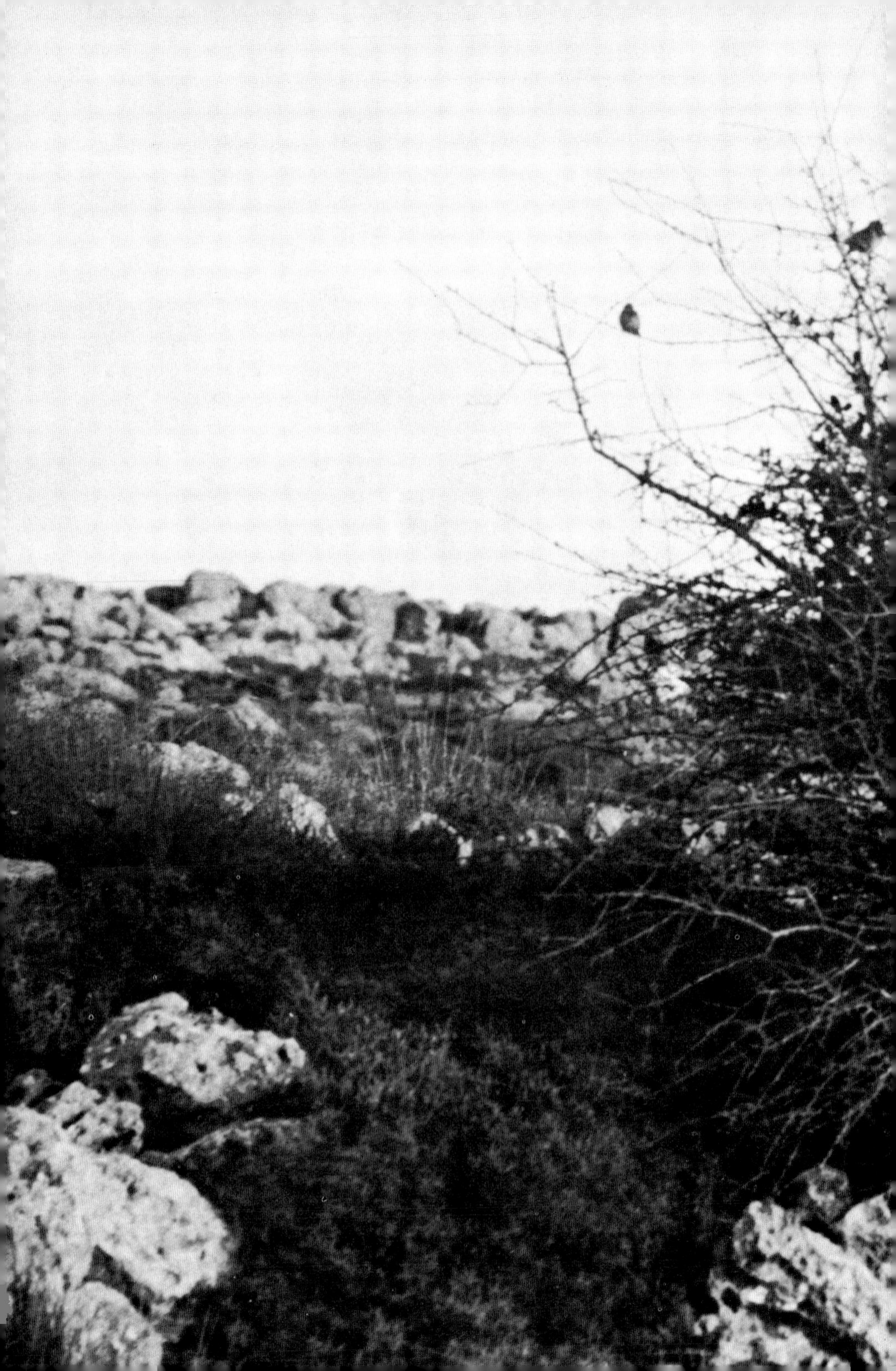

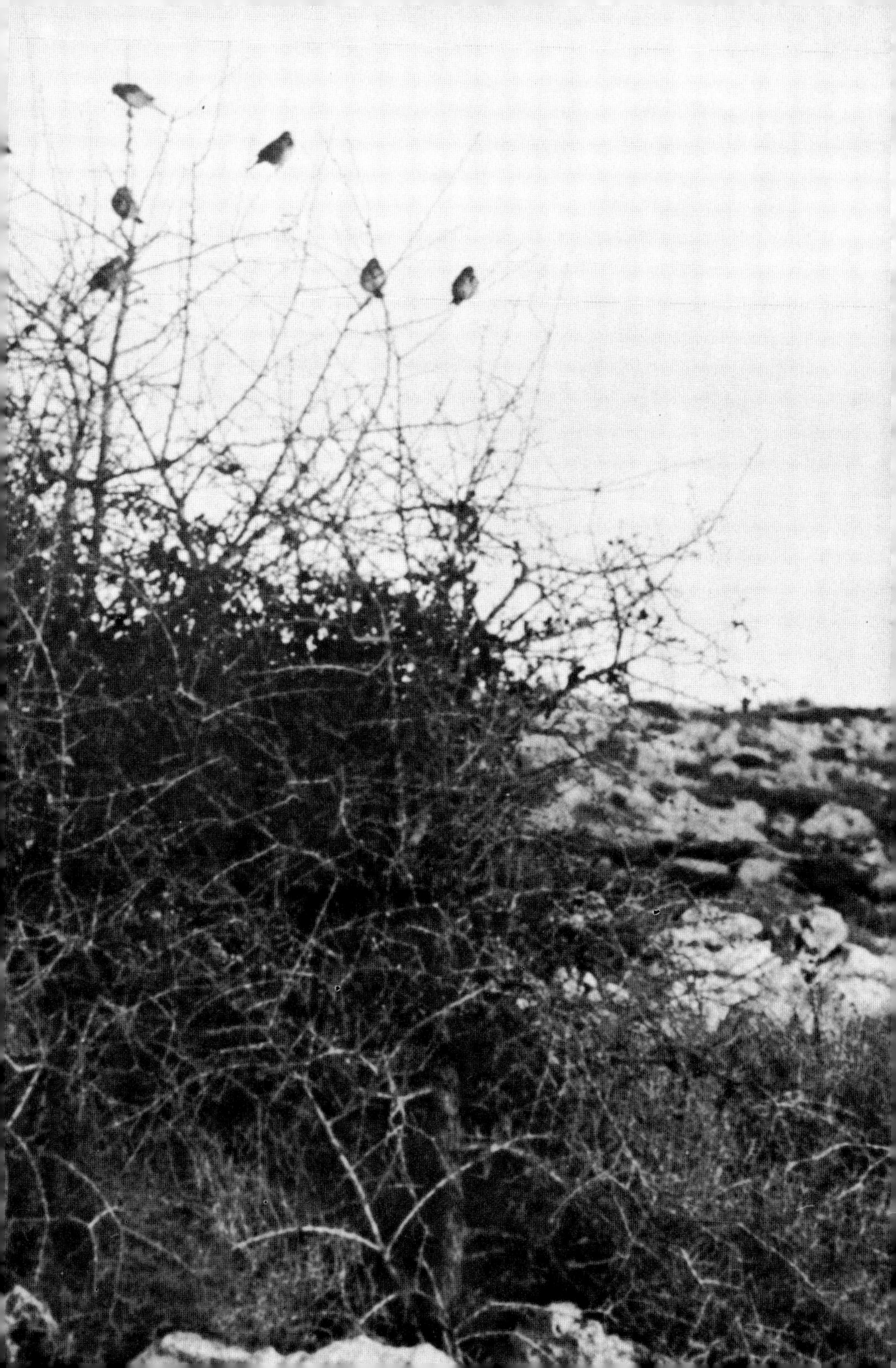

Cuckoo dipped her head, hiding her vulnerable face and eyes in the feathers of her chest. Though twice the size of Jay she bore the torrent of abuse without fighting back. Nothing would induce the stubborn cuckoo to leave this nest until she had accomplished her mission.

Jay was by now in a frenzy. She left off attacking the cuckoo and flew wildly about, berating the intruder loudly but making no new attempt to dislodge her. Jay's mate heard the cries and he too made a pass or two at the sitting cuckoo, then joined Jay in her tirade, screaming in frustration at the immobile nest thief.

Only when she had finished laying her egg did Cuckoo get up. Preening her feathers she gave a parting glance at the outraged jays and flew off. The jays were at first too exasperated to do more than scream abuse after the departing cuckoo but eventually got themselves under control and still complaining bitterly, they set about inspecting their newly-vacated property. A twig or two had been misplaced and they busied themselves with rearranging the nest. In their excitement neither noticed, nor perhaps could count well enough to discern that where one egg had reposed there were now two, one an exact replica of the other.

This egg, in the end, would be the source of a great deal of trouble for the unsuspecting jays. When the nestling cuckoo hatched, it would be twice the size of their own babies and would grow four times as fast. By the age of two weeks it would have pushed from the nest most of the true offspring of its foster parents and with its gaping maw always opened wide would get more than its share of the food. The two jays would be gaunt and tired before they finished with this chick and would be lucky indeed if they managed to provide enough food to keep even one of their own offspring alive.

The jays, unaware of the problems in store for them were content to get their nest back, and as Cuckoo flew off to seek tomorrows unwilling hosts, the jays were already rearranging their two eggs in the nest.

Polecat

POLECAT, exquisitely marbled in appearance was just waking up in a shallow hole under the bole of a fallen apple tree. It was an unusual hour for the polecat to waken but the last two days had been most unusual days. The most unusual in all the four months of his life. Polecat wakened slowly, a drowsy half-sleep still encompassed him as he let his ears and nose tell him the things he wanted to know. It was late afternoon of a warm spring day. There was the scent of pine-needles, of applewood and of decaying leaves. More than all there was the sharp smell of his own musk. The musk he had sprayed excessively the night before when he had been so frightened by all the sounds around him in the strangeness of his first night alone. The vague memory of last night's terror cut short his drowsy awakening and Polecat got up, sniffing around the new nest he had found and occupied the day before.

Until yesterday morning, Polecat had always been with his mother. Together with his brothers and sisters he had learned from her how to hunt and how to hide. Instinct had supplied much of his ability to fend for himself but the four months of instruction had helped equip him for life alone. For more than two weeks now, Polecat had been reluctant in his response to his mother's calls and yesterday, when he had failed to respond to her call she had left him, for she too knew that the time had come for Polecat to look for his own den in a new place. He was the first of his litter to do so but in the next two or three weeks, the others too would one by one go off to new places and live alone.

Peering out from under the trunk of the apple tree, Polecat gazed about him, partly to see if all was well, but partly to remember the landmarks of the place where he was sleeping. His sharp little eyes peered in all directions and his keen nose sniffed the air to detect the scent of danger, should danger be

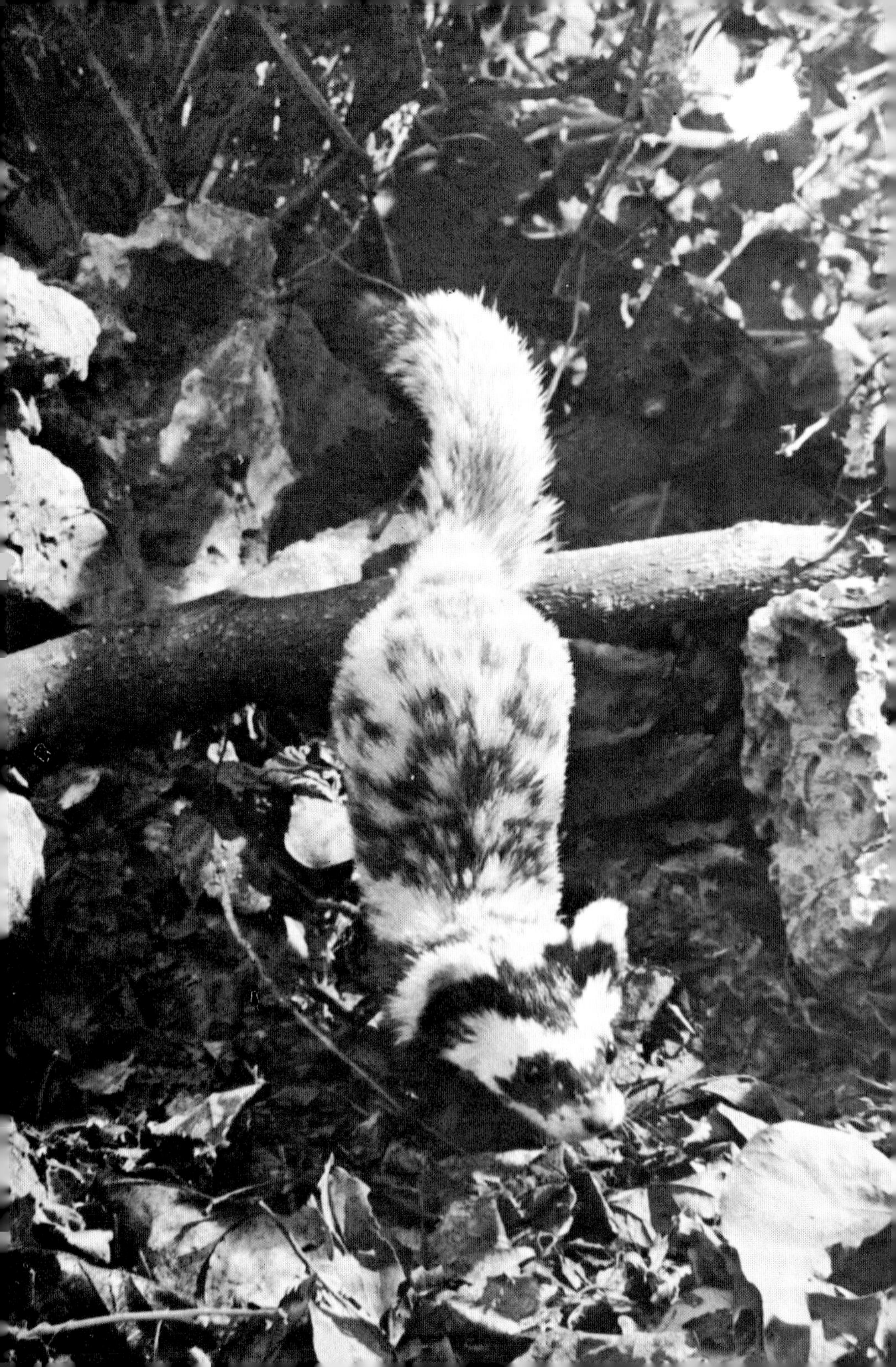

near his den. Three times he emerged from the hole under the log and each time the snapping of a twig or the rustle of a leaf sent him scuttling back; not turning but seemingly flowing backwards as his long body followed the bidding of his short legs and he reversed himself into the burrow again. At last, assured that the sounds about him were harmless, Polecat left the hole and stretched himself in the warm sunlight.

He was hungry, but hunger was not pressing him. Even a very young polecat knew that night was the time for hunting. Later he would seek among the terraces for the mice and beetles that would be his meal. More important at the moment was the musky scent on his fur which interfered with the keenness of his own sense of smell and would betray his presence to the animals he hunted.

A few dozen yards away he found the place he was looking for. He had visited it before with his mother and had remembered it the way he would always remember the places that were important to his well being. A large bank of earth, dark and rich with the remaining moisture of the winter rain still trapped in its fine grains would provide the bath he so desperately needed. Like all cats he was no lover of water and even had he been willing to enter it, water would have done little to remove the oil-based scent from his fur. Digging into the earthy bank, Polecat rolled himself in the fine loam, rubbing it into his pelt with his paws and covering himself completely with the dark richness of the earth.

In time, Polecat would save the use of his scent glands for real emergencies, just as he would learn not to scream himself hoarse at every imagined danger, the way he had last night. These two weapons were his only real defense, for he was small and though his sharp teeth served him well in killing small prey, they gave him no real protection. His musk was useful, for it stung like acid and the unlucky opponent that got a jet of it in his face was far too busy wiping his burning eyes to give chase, but more useful still was his voice. When Polecat was frightened, he screamed. His scream was so loud that even the bravest enemy was taken aback that such a sound could come from so tiny a creature as Polecat, and in the moment of surprise Polecat usually would be gone leaving a cloud of his offensive perfume behind him.

His earth-bath finished, Polecat sat grooming his silky three-colored pelt. His nose told him that now his scent was fresh and sweet with the smell of fresh soil pervading. Rubbing his tiny paws over his ears, then licking them to wash his face, Polecat was busy with his ablutions until the dusk began to gather. Stretching himself from his reverie, Polecat set out for his evening's hunting.

Halfway down the slope to the terraces, a pine-cone clattered noisily to the ground, falling a few inches from his nose. Polecat leapt aside, his tail erect but he neither screamed nor gave off scent. Polecat was growing up.

Mantis

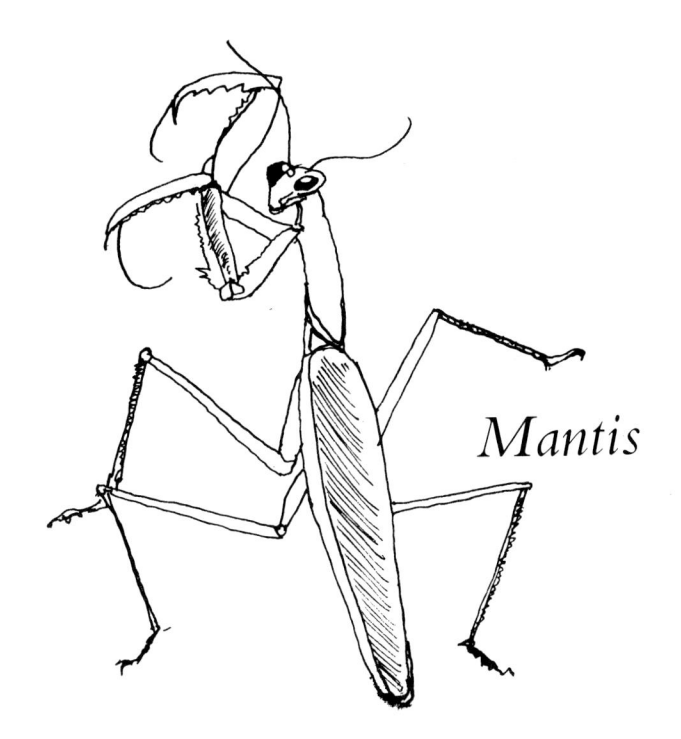

Mantis was there, before the wadi was there. When the first rains cut into the hills, beginning the eons of work that would create the contours of this place, a mantis, no different from those that would follow her, laid her eggs in a water-tight pouch and then died. The next spring had seen the dozen or so of her children foraging in the bush for their sustenance.

Mantis was young. She was just past her fourth moult and another six months would pass before she too would mate with a male of her kind in the pomegranate tree and would lay her eggs in their pouch on one of the branches of this very tree where she herself was hatched. When her eggs had been laid, she too would feel her life force abating and in the cool of a November night she would fall into a stupor and waken no more.

Mantis was a huntress. Her stick-like body was perfectly camouflaged in this, her natural habitat and her forefeet were a cunning instrument for catching other insects which she held daintily, nibbling them with her sharp mouth-parts and letting their chitinous wings and carapaces fall messily to the ground below. Only the shrew, that tiny mammalian predator of the forest floor could match her when it came to appetite. Several times her weight in food-stuffs found their way into her greedy mouth each day, yet she was always hungry after a few minutes.

Mantis lived in a large pomegranate tree grown wild. It had been planted in the days when man had been about and for many years the mantis had lived there. Mantis, hatching from her pod among the leaf branches, had never left the tree. The pomegranate blossoms and the sweet resin of the tree served as a trap for the insects she desired and Mantis, her needs provided for, never had had reason to hunt elsewhere.

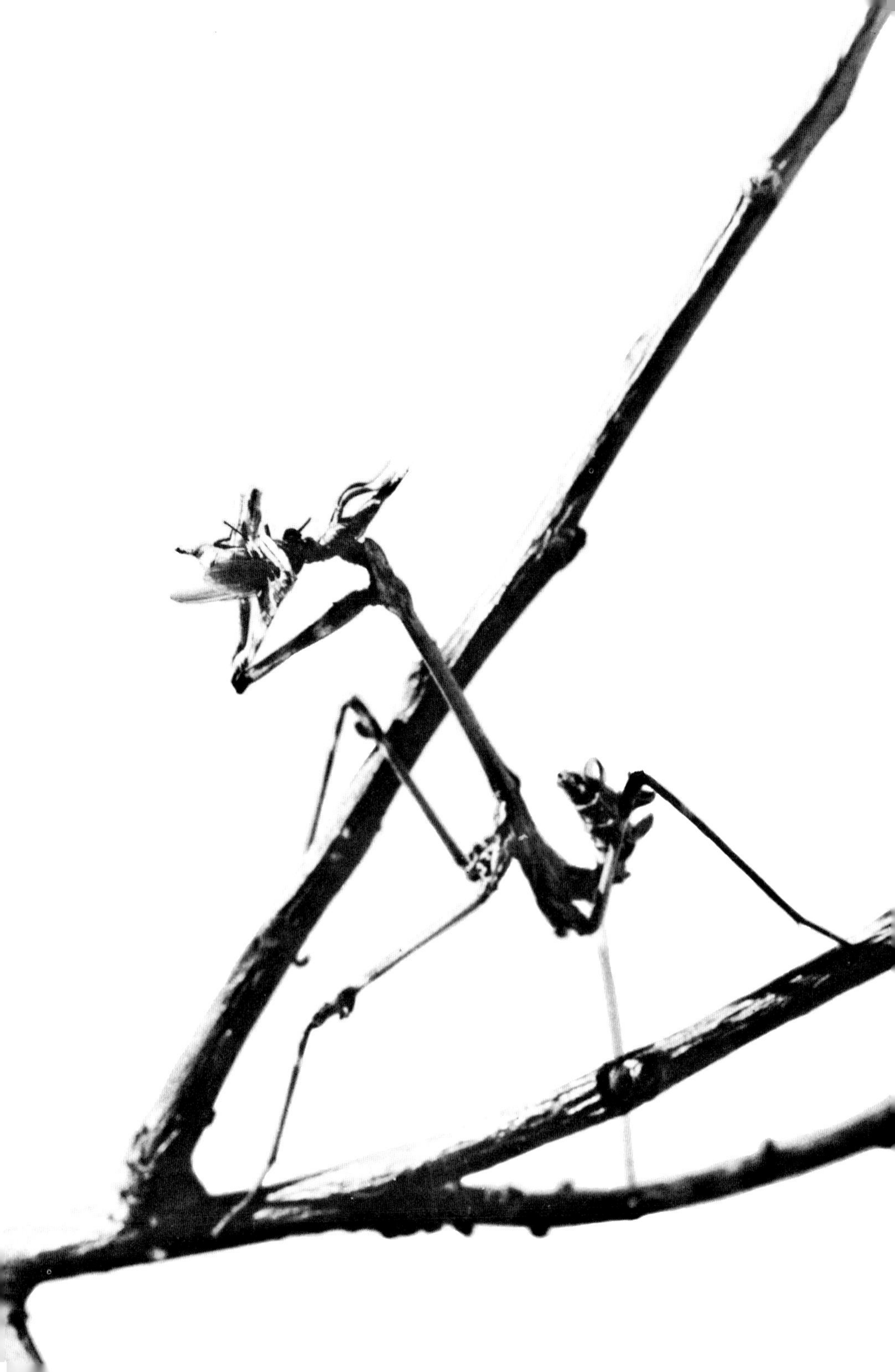

She had eaten most of her brothers and sisters in the course of time, and even now, any mantis straying into her realm might well find itself the hunted rather than the hunter. Only during the breeding season would she tolerate the presence of a courting male and even he had more than a fifty per cent chance of being devoured by his bride once her eggs were fertilized. Although the late autumn always saw a few males still alive when the females had all laid their eggs and died, these

males were the rare survivors who had either not mated at all or had managed to escape the quick jaws of their chosen female.

Mantis, warm in the spring air, sat on a twig near a pomegranate flower. Without bestirring herself unduly she plucked a fat beetle from the edge of the flower and munched him as she sat. Her hunger assuaged for a moment, Mantis sat quietly in the sunshine, folding her legs in the prayerful attitude of a mantis at rest.

Epilogue

THE WADI is changing now. Forces of which the animals are unaware, and could not in any case understand, are turning the wadi into a wilderness.

Each year the wild-life becomes less abundant as the wadi becomes less habitable, for the creatures that live in Addulam are hardy in the biological sense, yet unprepared for the countless dangers that beset them in the modern world that man has made.

A road loops the wadi now, cutting across the grassy plateau on the road to the spring and rare is the motorist who will sacrifice a few miles per hour to save the life of an animal. As a result, there is scarcely a night when one of the familiar denizens of the area does not die on its way to or from the life-giving spring down below.

The planted fields of man must be protected from predatory insects and they are sprayed with insecticides, often excessively and without proper attention to wind velocity or direction. Half of the poison is sprayed, not on the cherished crops, but into the wadi wilderness, poisoning food and water sources essential to life.

Even nature lovers, intrepid in their search for the unspoiled beauty of the countryside are careless and uninformed. Plastic bags, filled with scraps from the picnic table, are left behind, the owner consoled by the knowledge that he did not litter the area but had put the bag under a stone. But the stone is overturned, the parcel devoured, and a gazelle or other animal dies in agony of an intestinal obstruction. The man made material, synthesized with scientific skill is indigestible.

As the animals that prey on mice die out, the mice multiply. In desperation, the farmers poison with greater vigor and more eagles, falcons, badgers, hedgehogs and polecats die of the poisons. The cycle feeds upon its own results and the end can only be disaster, for the animals and eventually for man, the catalyst who has set it in motion.

In the end, only Viper remains, deadly and invulnerable. Unharmed by poisons, he lives on with no mongoose, eagle or hedgehog to challenge his kingship in the wadi.

But there are other wadis where man has not yet set in motion the forces of destruction. They may still be saved, but only if we understand that the lack of a desire to destroy will not protect. Today, since most of our depradations are collective, there must be an active will to preserve. It is not enough to wish no harm to living things. One must also wish them well.

Only an awakened public, willing to sacrifice a little time and questionable short-term gains can create the laws needed to protect the last remaining strongholds of our vanishing wild-life. Only citizens who cherish not only the land but all that is therein can take the action necessary to protect the heritage of their children and the generations that are to come.

There are still wadis like the wadi in this book. It is not too late to save them. Not yet.

Temple Israel
Library
Minneapolis, Minn.

יהי אור

LET THERE BE LIGHT

In honor of
the Bar Mitzvah of
Gregg Moral
by
Dr. & Mrs. Harvey M. Moral & Family